# Compulsive Lying In Relationships

**The Comprehensive Guide to Building Trust and Emotional Intimacy**

**David Joseph**

No part of this publication may be reproduced, or transmitted in any form or by any means including photocopying, recording or other electronics or mechanical method without the prior permission of the publisher except for brief quotations embodied in critical reviews.

**ISBN:** 9781796422856

# Table of Contents

# Dedication

This book is dedicated to my wife, Debbie, and all those who love the truth.

# Preface

If you expect the trust of someone, you must come clean and demonstrate honesty and integrity from the beginning and maintain it throughout the entire relationship. You get what you give in a relationship. Trust and honesty are necessarily the key ingredients of any successful relationship. Promoting trust is crucial in building a strong, healthy relationship between two people. Honesty fosters trust. If you come clean and honest, and you don't keep your partner in the dark about important things that they might want to know, it is most likely you get the same treatment back. Therefore, if you imbibe honesty and communicate your feelings openly and freely to your partner then you're likely going to get the same type of treatment back from your partner. Keeping secrets from your partner can compromise your trust and lead to a breaking down of the cohesiveness in your relationship.

Love may have been the primary key to starting the relationship, but being trustworthy to your partner will be the main thing to keep and sustain it. Honesty in everything is a critical component of a healthy relationship. Being honest in everything helps us avoid damaging breaches of trust and allows us to live in reality as opposed to fantasy. Relationships where both people care about improving the rapport, strive to better themselves, and love one another, tend to be successful. Although issues may arise, but they are always ready to team up and nip things in the bud before it escalates. Even if they argue or disagree on things, they are committed to an earlier resolution. It takes hard work to maintain a healthy relationship, when we are honest with ourselves and our partner, you will experience the joy and excitement of living in a genuine relationship. Honesty in relationships makes us feel safe and secure because we know where we stand by talking about our concerns always and sharing things openly with one another.

Not everything we experience in a relationship will be warm and rosy. But, if there is a steady flow of *give and take*, willingness to be truthful, in spite of challenges, there will be cohesion in the relationship. We can conveniently handle much anything that arises, as long as we are willing to live in reality and face the truths. Healthy and vibrant relationships are built on openness and mutual trust. When trust is lost, it gives way for distrust and misunderstanding. Deceit is a common problem with many people nowadays affecting their happiness and choices. Relationships that are healthy, cheery and balanced are characterized by real people who are in touch with their authentic selves. It is hard to give what you don't have; honesty begins with you. You should consider the potential damage and complications that surround lying before you indulge in the habit. If you wish to enjoy a healthy relationship, you have to stop lying, live uprightly, and treat your partner with respect and dignity.

This book offers a sound and reliable roadmap to building trust and emotional intimacy in a relationship. You will learn about what you can do to promote an atmosphere of honesty around you and generate a steady flow of trust in your relationship.

Compulsive Lying in Relationships

# 1 The Truth about Lying

Deceits and lies endanger trust and can damage us and our relationships—sometimes irreparably. The habits of lying are such a big part of our modern society that it's nearly commonplace affairs nowadays. Lying may appear harmless and straightforward at first, but just like any addiction, you'll soon find yourself trapped and overwhelmed more than you could have ever imagined, and in the process, you damage your relationships, lose your integrity, and burn numerous bridges. Lying is one of the quickest ways to ruin a beautiful relationship.

It often begins with the intention of gaining attention, boost self-esteem, or to increase social standing. However, over

1

time the opposite often results. Because according to an old saying. *A lie may take care of the present, but it has no future.*

Most People will tell you that lying is ethically wrong. But in reality, when it comes to avoiding trouble or sparing someone's feelings, many people easily fall into it. Lying is toxic to relationships of all kinds. When you lie, thinking your partner will never find out, you will almost certainly create a barrier of hurt in your relationship because, when the other person finds out about your deceit, and they usually do, it's virtually impossible to regain trust. Because once you are caught in one lie, it makes people question everything you are saying whether genuine or fake. The habits of lying and deception in a relationship or marriage

2

can be tricky because it often leads to a loss of trust and it makes other people feel less concerned about each other. The best way to destroy trust in a relationship is by getting caught deceiving your partner. It can lead to a loss of trust and confidence and increased distance between partners. These problems are made much worse when deception actually comes open.

It is not possible to have a close, healthy relationship without mutual trust. Relationships often come to an end when someone gets caught lying. You need to be able to depend on your partner and trust what they tell you. The more you engage in dishonesty with your partner, the more you tend to feel less close to them which weaken the cord of unity. It is hard to believe that your partner knows you, and understands you if you are always lying to him or her. The more we lie to people, the less we trust them. We project our deceptive tendencies on to others.

Although we may consider ourselves to be honest, few of us reveal all our negative thoughts and feelings to our partner. It requires strong courage to be vulnerable and genuine. In a close relationship, honesty includes allowing our partner to know who we are. Sincerity is more than just not lying. Deception includes making vague statements, manipulating information through unnecessary emphasis, exaggeration, or telling half-truths. It also covers minimization and withholding information that is important to someone who has a right to know, because it affects the cohesiveness of a

4

relationship and deprives the victim of freedom of choice and informed decision. Lying to a husband or wife even when it is not detected, can cause problems.

Discovering that your partner has lied, especially about an important issue, is a very emotionally painful experience. It can be challenging to deal with, because it raises many questions about the relationship. When a spouse gets caught in deceit, it raises suspicion, which causes people to re-evaluate their partner as well as their commitment to the relationship. It is therefore not surprising that relationships sometimes end in divorce when deception comes to light. Because most people find it hard and extremely difficult to get over an intimate partner's betrayal.

Reasons People Lie

There are wide ranges of reasons why people tell lies in a relationship. Some of the reasons include;

The thought of protection: The thought of protection is one of the main reasons why people engage in deceitful habits. It can be protection for others and protection for oneself.

Protection of oneself is driven by fear of criticism, loss of respect, or to hide true feelings or compensate for the reality. In some cases, it can be driven by a fear of punishment; this is especially common with children when kids try to hide the truth to evade being punished.

The second form; Protection for others is born out of avoiding hurting people's feelings. The liar often believes that if they tell the individual the truth, it will probably hurt their feelings or will in some way be detrimental to them. They are of the view that telling the truth may bring out hidden secrets that can damage their relationship.

Personal gain: This includes manipulating others or a situation to make gains. This could be financial gain or any other form of benefit.

Little white lies: People tell so many white lies they hardly recognize themselves doing it at all. These are common lies that we often overlooked. For example, telling someone, we are okay (when in reality we are not).

Sometimes, emotional fear causes people to lie. Most people's lies stem from a desire to self-preserve in some way. They are not necessarily lying to deceive, but to protect their own ego. Maybe they have already disappointed in one way or the other, and they are afraid of the consequences and the likely reaction from their partners. They're ashamed of what they have done and need to cover the act not to disappoint their partner when the matter is known. People in this type of case often justify themselves that they're not really lying. Although. This is a mild case of dishonesty which we may perceive as not harmful. But regardless of the reasons for deception, the habit of lying is a toxic practice that can eventually break down your relationship. If you deliberately tell a lie to avoid hurting someone else and preserve yourself, that is intentionally hiding your own behavior. When you hide your true identity, you are indirectly violating the right of your partner to make his/her personal choice about the acceptability of your behavior.

Compulsive Lying in Relationships

## 2 Seemingly Harmless White Lies That Can Ruin Your Relationship

Little white lies that seem harmless can actually do some severe damage to any relationship. Little lies unaddressed can get out of hand and prevent you from addressing larger relationship issues. Lie builds up gradually and subtly developed into big issues. Telling white lies or hiding even the smallest things from your partner will probably not going to help your relationship, therefore, it shouldn't be tolerated in any way. People sometimes hide things from their partner or claim to be telling these small lies for a few different reasons. Or, they may deliberately be doing something that they probably shouldn't be doing and are using the crook means by lying or hiding it from their partner. Little lies may appear non-trivial issue initially but can turn into something much bigger In the long run. Being honest with your partner is the best option — even if it means things are getting a little prickly. Your relationship will suffer and struggle to survive if it is not built on integrity.

According to Richard Feynman *"The first principle is that you must not fool yourself—and you are the easiest person to fool."*

Small lies such as, 'It doesn't bother me,' its fine or I'm fine, can easily damage a relationship. Masking your feelings and pretending that all is well when the reverse is the case can have a long term damaging effect on your relationship. Maybe you feel it is of no use talking it out with your partner just to keep the relationship going. Saying all is well when you are hurt within, won't take the problem away. Pretending that you are not bothered by the action of your partner that isn't satisfying can later resurface. It can come up later during an argument from something that is not related. Being honest with yourself is crucial, to be honest with your partner. Healthy and vibrant relationships are built on honesty. No relationship can survive, let alone thrive, without openness and integrity.

Here are some seemingly harmless little lies that can actually ruin your relationship if care is not taken.

*Lies about finances are trust breakers.*

It's imperative to be open about financial problems and not just brush it aside. Many people find a discussion about money awkward. The truth is money is a crucial factor in any relationship. A lot of people struggle to meet up financially, so if all is not well financially don't hide it to your partner. Let your partner be aware of your situation financially. If you lie about your finance, your debt, or your spending habits, prepare for problems.

*Lying about ex*

Lying about an ex is the worst lie you can tell to your partner. If you have any encounter with your ex, come open and don't hide it from your partner. Even if it is an innocent exchange of words, your partner deserves to know to clear any suspicion. The issue of infidelity can be very devastating to any relationship.

## Lying about sex

Don't lie to your partner about your feelings concerning sex. Remember, you deserve to feel sexually satisfied — and your partner wants that too. If you aren't in the mood let your partner know, it is not compulsory you must be in the spirit always. However, it should be an open conversation. Telling little lies to evade sex can hurt your partner and create distance between the two of you.

## *Inability to accept being wrong*

We all make mistakes. Failure to take responsibility for errors can make things go wrong in a relationship. Some people find it difficult to take responsibility for even the smallest things, but instead, they will deny and spin lies to cover up. If you are unwilling or unable to admit when you are wrong, they are going to put your relationship at risk.

# 3 How to Stop Lying to Yourself

We are susceptible to self-deception because we have special emotional attachments to our beliefs. Our personal opinion is often accepted as truth. And before we are even aware, we become obsessed and try to convince others of the conviction by creating an excellent description around those beliefs. Getting caught up in the web of your own lies can lessen your sense of self-respect distort your perception of reality and impact your relationship negatively. If you are not honest with yourself, how will you ever be honest with someone else? Relationships that are healthy, happy and balanced are characterized by real people who are in touch with their authentic selves. It is hard to give what you don't have; honesty begins with you.

Be welcoming to honest advice

Don't just dismiss constructive criticism from people who meant well. If you are given a bit of honest, somewhat critical assessment that seems to contradict your view, you shouldn't be so quick to dismiss it. Don't see it as a personal attack but an opportunity for self-examination. You should be able to differentiate an overly critical person and an honest and helpful friend who is willing to give a useful advice.

Consider others' points of view.

Before you conclude and get upset at someone for doing something you perceived as improper, stop and try to consider their reasoning. Don't judge hastily or see yourself as always right. Listening to their story and try to visualize it from their angle will help you to see things in clear perspective. It may be possible they had good reasons that you merely overlooked. When you disrespect others point of viewpoint using defensiveness, victimization, anger, you are lying to yourself because your reactions are defense mechanisms. Instead of winning them over by force to your point of view try to present your view in constructive ways that help and nurture others to convince them.

Stop saying yes when you don't really mean it.

Don't be a yes man always. Stop saying yes when you actually mean no. Some people feel obliged to say "yes" to others for all sorts of reasons even to their personal detriment. If saying yes isn't being true to caring for your particular needs and time resources, then it's important to be realistic and say outright no instead of yes to please other people. It's good for other people to learn that you're standing up for yourself. Don't do or say things just because other people do or expect you to. Contorting yourself to meet others' expectations will erode your individuality, and dampen your morale. Learning when to say no is an essential skill and happiness tool.

Don't ignore your feelings.

Don't ignore your feelings, acknowledge when you're scared or deeply overwhelmed by things. Lies often stem from the desire for self-protection. We often tell lies when we want to protect ourselves. The willingness to self-protection is a response to something that we fear. The more you acknowledge your fears, the less you'll see the need to lie for a cover-up.

Recognize when you're exaggerating your abilities and accomplishments

Exaggerating your abilities will prevent you from being true to yourself. This type of lies to yourself will eventually cause you confusion, frustration. People will begin to doubt your reputation when they discover that you can't keep up in the way you said you would. Learn to be humble and share your vulnerabilities with other people rather than hiding it. This helps people to understand yourself better and make you look genuine in their eyes.

Be wary of your inability to keep up with your words.

Be wary of living on empty promises when you tell yourself that things are going to change, but you are not prepared for it. Saying that you'd like things to be different is one thing. Doing something to make it happen is another thing. If you want things to change, you must map out concrete steps of action for yourself and really work towards achieving it.

Otherwise, things will be exactly the same as they are. Don't sit back passively expecting the changes to come overnight, only your action and determination can make the desired difference.

## Be more truthful to yourself

Be alert to the need to be more self-righteousness by holding yourself to a high standard of internal truth-telling. It will probably take some effort and practice, but once you form the habit, you'll catch yourself when you lie to yourself and start stopping it from happening. Things will begin to fall in place favorably as you are more truthful to yourself. You'll develop a real understanding of your limitations and trust yourself the more. You will become much more confident in yourself. Being honest with yourself makes you a brave and fearless individual. You have a deeper understanding of yourself, and don't believe you need to change that. When you are connected to your core values, you are less bothered by other negative perception of you. This is essential to know what you want. You don't feel the need to judge others or gossip about them, as your personal security makes you accepting of yourself and others. Don't build your character on the unpredictable foundation of public opinion. You have to be able to rely on yourself to pursue what you want.

# 4 How Secrets and Lies Destroy Relationships

A relationship needs trust to thrive continuously. Trust is a fundamental element of a stable relationship. When trust is lost in a relationship, it gives way for distrust and misunderstanding. Deceit can be one of the quickest ways to strip that needed trust from a relationship. It is a widespread problem with many people nowadays affecting their happiness and choices.

The way we manage guilt and dishonesty acts generate more problems. We mask our feelings and hide our true identity in order to keep the secret. We rationalize our lie or deceit to avoid the inner conflict, and the danger we imagine awaits us if we speak the truth. Some people become obsessed with deceit, to the extent that they will lie about everything. They can be so compelling that they are convinced that lying supports their relationship. They are not ready to face the hurt or choices that the truth could precipitate. They have difficulty concentrating on anything else. The potential damage and complications that surround lying are things to consider when telling lies.

Most liars worry about the risks of being truthful but give little attention to the risks of dishonesty. However, lying is a slow killer of a relationship and affects relationships of all kinds.

Some ways by which lies and deceits can cause harm are discussed below.

Lie blocks cordiality with a partner. A good relationship needs mutual trust and intimacy to thrive. Affection is based on reliance, openness, and genuineness. Lies lead to suspicion and being suspicious makes it extremely difficult for any relationship to flourish. Cordiality is based on mutual trust, even if that trust is, from time to time, somewhat misplaced.

## Lies Erode Trust

The foundation for a flourishing and robust relationship is built on mutual trust and understanding. Lies and trust cannot coexist; lies erode trust, and without trust, there's no relationship. When trust is lost, the chances of maintaining a healthy relationship is low; total collapse is imminent. Lies can utterly damage the foundation of a relationship and make it unbefitting for one or both parties. Once there is no trust your interaction suffers, and doubts begin to replace trust that once exists in the relationship. You become suspicious of the person and begin to live in expectation of future untruths from that person. *When you lie once, you make it that much difficult to believe you even when you're telling the truth, your words and actions become questionable.*

## Feeling of guilt

In most cultures, honesty is valued as a moral norm, although the context and specifics may differ. When we run against religious or cultural norms by being dishonest and hide the truth, we experience anxiety generated by the feeling of guilt. Over time, the deception can eat away at our self-esteem; undermining your fundamental sense of dignity.

## Lying Demonstrates Selfishness

The habit of Lying can be an indication of selfishness and disregard for the other party in a relationship. When you lie, you are basically putting personal self-interest above that of your partner. Unwillingness to make a sacrifice for the higher, long-term good of a relationship put strains on the relationship. Acting without consideration for the interest of the other party makes the other party feel insignificant. This can lead to less commitment and eventually the collapse of the relationship. The fact of the matter is that for a relationship to thrive, both parties must be able to trust each other.

Lies can systematically permeate the other aspects of your life.

Lies can permeate other aspects of your life without you even knowing it. No one tells just one lie; you need more lies to support one lie. It is a dangerous cycle to fall into as the say goes thus *one lie often leads to another and a liar is always a liar.* There is a tendency to want to be evasive every time you find yourself in a sticky situation especially if you have gotten away with a few already. The fact of the matter is that when you lie for the first time and gets away with it, you become invincible and so you are more likely to want to lie even more. Telling lies become more comfortable, and before you know it, lies begin to manifest in all aspects of your life. You begin to lie on the job and even among friends. There is a tendency to want to be evasive every time you find yourself in a sticky situation because for you telling a lie is more comfortable than telling the truth. The habit then begins to evolve and becomes a problem when you tell too many lies as these lies may become difficult to contain. As times goes on it becomes addictive and keeping your story straight becomes a serious challenge.

## Feeling a Fool for Believing a Lie

When you lied, and it becomes open, your partner becomes upset, feeling being fooled forever falling for the deceit. The agony of the deceit will perpetually change his perception. The ugly experience may create permanent cracks in the wall of your relationship which can erode any sense of cohesiveness that once existed in the relationship. The affected person may feel cheated and maltreated and spend all his time plotting to hit back and revenge. If you were to be at the receiving end, you would not tolerate your partner going around lying to you, no matter how small the lies may seem to be.

When someone you love and trust with all of your heart lies to you, it creates feelings of misunderstanding, betrayal, and sadness which can result in devastating sorrow. Furthermore, it can limit your progress, hinder your life goals, and make you literally sick.

Lies Create a Sense of Imbalanced

For a relationship to work there should be a balance of effort from both parties; they must give equal commit and commitment to it. This balance of effort creates the feeling of trust and understanding that strengthened a relationship. On the other hand, lying upset the flow of this natural equilibrium and causes an imbalance in the relationship. For the victim of a lie, the experience can be devastating and make them feel as though they have put their all their heart on the line, only to be disappointed by a deceptive partner.

## Lying Shows a Lack of Respect

Lying shows a lack of respect and distrust. As soon as lack of respect manifests in a relationship, it begins to put a strain on all aspects of the relationship and, if left unchecked, it can damage the relationship. When your partner lied to you, you have a feeling of disrespect from your partner. It proves that the other your partner does not place a significant value upon the relationship. Being told the truth confers the feeling of respect upon the recipient and shows that the other person is not prepared to endanger the relationship by deceiving them. The other partner may begin to react to the avoidant behavior by feeling perplexed, disbelieving, worried, deprived, angry or neglected. He/she may begin to suspect the other partner, and their self-esteem may suffer. The victims of betrayal often require counseling to get over the loss of trust and boost the lost trust and confidence. Partners should try to maintain an open and honest dialogue about their feelings and their relationship. When we treat our partner with respect and sincerity, we are true not only to them but to ourselves. We can plan and make decisions about our lives and our actions without compromising our integrity or acting suspiciously.

## Lying cause unnecessary apprehension

Beyond breaking trust, telling lies can cause uneasiness in a relationship. When your partner has to always worry about you lying or hiding things from them and struggle to decipher truth from lies Because of the pattern of lying he hardly knows the difference between your truths and lies. This induces unnecessary fear and anxiety that he/she possibly would not have had if it wasn't for you lying to him in the first place. The feeling is that, if you lie about the small things, you are likely to lie about bigger things. These are uncertainties your partner will now carry with them, and with good reason. Nobody likes to be lied to.

## Health issues

When the truth comes out, it can be devastating and traumatic to realize that the one we loved and trust has betrayed us. It can shatter the image we have of our partner, as well as the confidence in ourselves and even reality itself. Research evidence shows that such discovery can lead to health issues apart from common mental distress. The thought of disappointment on the victim can cause considerable damage. Research evidence shows that happily married couples experience a number of physical and mental health benefits because of the feeling of affection, appreciation, or warm personal attachment. This type of intimacy encourages personal satisfaction, prosperity, long and fruitful

37

life. On the other hand, lying can impact this intimacy by negatively affects all parts involved- the liar and the victim. Unexpected traumatic event can cause unusual reactions, illness, as well as stress and uncertainties.

## 5 Reasons to Stop Lying and Save Your Relationship

Lying does nothing good for a relationship, it only prolongs issues and makes situation get worse on the long run. No matter which way you may try to spin it, lying doesn't solve anything; it causes people to act differently and tends to undermine the bond that holds relationships together. Lying is a stressful behavior, and nobody wants to be friends with a liar. Liars can't be trusted, and they hurt other people with their lies. If you desire a long lasting relationship in your life, you need to stop lying and be trustworthy.

You will find that it is an excellent relief, to tell the truth. *If you tell the truth, it becomes a part of your past. If you tell a lie, it becomes a part of your future.*

Abraham Lincoln said: *"If you once forfeit the confidence of your fellow citizens, you can never regain their respect and esteem."*

When you lie, you hurt your mind and make yourself out of touch with reality. You disguise and project deceit and falsehood to your partner. He/she may not know that you are telling lies, but right within, you know the truth because you can only lie to people but not yourself. The guilt of deceit will hang on unless you decide to change and come out clean. If you wish to develop a healthy relationship you have to treat your partner with respect and dignity, you have to stop lying and live uprightly.

Lying won't solve problems

According to Tad Williams *"We tell lies when we are afraid... afraid of what we don't know, afraid of what others will think, afraid of what will be found out about us. But every time we tell a lie, the thing that we fear grows stronger'*. Lying won't solve problems. It can only provide momentary satisfaction which will fade away with time. It may cover the shame and the guilt for the moment, but will not render a realistic solution to the problem. The moment you realize this vital point the good for you to seek to eradicate lies from your life before it wreaks uncontrollable havoc.

When your interpersonal relationship suffers, you become the worse person to look up to when someone is trying to solve a problem.

Lying hurts the ones you care about the most.

Lying hurts the ones we care about the most, sometimes when we lie, we do so to get ourselves out of a sticky situation. We may not mean to harm our partners. But in reality, lies do hurt. By concealing the truth, you are depriving your partner necessary information, and when the truth is known, they will feel betrayed by you. The feeling of betrayer can lead to a breakdown in communication which can create a crack in the cohesiveness of a relation. Love doesn't hurt, but lies do; and the moment you start telling lies, it is no longer love.

## Lying has serious consequences

Some people believe that little lies do not matter. They opined that telling a lie, especially a little white one has no effect and nothing will become of it. They become obsessed with their lie, that they are convinced that lying supports the relationship. But that is not usually the case. Lying cannot solve problems; it is only temporary relief. Lies have both seen and unforeseen consequences when they are uncovered, some of which can be life-changing. However, you may believe that there are several levels of lying, but the painful truth is that the ones you hurt suffer emotionally.

Lie causes misunderstanding between you and your partner

Telling lies keep you from addressing the real issue. You may assume things are all right, but in reality, your partner is feeling the effect of your action. When you think you've made amends with your apologies, your partner may find it challenging to cope fully, and it may take quite a while for them to move on from it. They will ever remember how you were able to manipulate them until you got caught. Even if your misunderstanding is about other issues, those lies readily come to memory. They will resurface one way or another especially if the lie is about something of great importance that will stay with the relationship for a long time.

## 6 How to Stop Lying and save your relationship

Lies can hurt other people and damage a relationship when all the truths are showed off. Most people believe lying is better than the truth because it seems to be the easiest way out in comparison with the confronting the truth. Lying is more comfortable and pleasant to the ear. But the fact is every time you lie; you create a crack in the wall of a relationship because lying is a temporary solution to a permanent problem. Lying is a terribly destructive habit, if you wish to have a guilt-free life, if you want to live with respect and dignity; you have to stop lying to yourself and others. Whenever you begin to eradicate the cause and the result of your lying habit, your relationships and self-worth might be improved. Learning to be honest and seeking the truth with yourself and your partner is the more proactive approach to happy living. Honesty is the simplest thing you can practice to be happy, prosperous and fulfilled. Honesty improves our vitality, endears us to friends and loved ones. It engenders confidence, strengthens our willpower and represents us in the best way for others to emulate. Being honest with yourself is a great way to build trust, rise above life challenges, gain self-acceptance, and develop genuineness for a healthy relationship.

Begin to see things from your partner's point of view. Think about the effect of your action on your partner, if it were to be the other way round, how would you have felt. Would you like to be cheated by your partner? When you consider this factor you will empathize more with their precarious position each time you cheat. Once you start lying, you put your partner in a dangerous situation, because someone has to be at the receiving end of your act of dishonesty. You may not even be able to determine the enormous effect of a small lie or the danger that it holds not just for you but your partner. Consider the implication of lying on your relationship. Will you be able to face a situation of losing the trust and respect of your partner? Can you stand the risk of breaking up with your partner? Even if you break up, your future will also be doomed because of your deception and lack of integrity. You should avoid this

49

problem by being honest with your partner and the people around you. Here are some things you can do to save your relationship from the damaging effects of lying

## Admit your problems

Stop justifying yourself that you are always right, and that you have every reason to lie. Admit that you have problems. This is always the first, significant, and most challenging step to put the situation under control. The very fact that you suspect that your partner may be neglecting you, disrespecting you or even has taken you for granted is not sufficient to keep lying to your partner. The wrongdoings of your partner shouldn't justify your lies. Stop self-deception and be honest with yourself. Admitting and open up to your partner about your problem will create a chance for both of you to work towards creating an enduring change. You will realize that there is no need to look completely perfect for your partner.

## Remind yourself how lying ruin and messes up your life.

The consequences of lying can be devastating, Lying destroys relationships and adds terrific trouble to your life. Take the time to consider what the consequences are going to be if you continue the bad habit. From your knowledge so far, has it been a great experience ever to keep up telling lies? Some lies may have given you nightmares when you thought of the consequences of getting caught.

Analyze the root cause

If you want to give up lying, you need to find out what pressured you to lie. Has the habit been beneficial in any to you or the person you lied to. You need to ask yourself, what am I trying to hide? What would have been a better way, to tell the truth? These are critical issues you need to examine before you can get yourself out of this embarrassing situation.

Personal respect

Personal respect is something that you need to cultivate to understand the value of your words. Often, liars don't recognize

52

how their actions hurt their own reputation. They enjoy manipulating others to get the best out of every situation. But when you understand your worth, you will want to refrain from what can lead you to an embarrassing situation. Compulsive lying can snowball into a personality disorder and because you know you aren't able to keep your word strait, you can start to think less of yourself.

Practice telling the truth.

Be honest in all your conversation and do not compromise by integrating the truth with lies. When you start feeling the urge to lie, stop and think for a moment. Think about what your partner would feel about you if they knew you were lying. Think about the implication of the action on your partner and the relationship. A real relationship is when you can tell each other anything and everything. No secrets and no lies. Practice telling the truth. Do not compromise by adding, removing or integrating the truth with dishonesty. Honesty, regardless of how bad it tastes, is a critical factor that determines the strength of your intimacy.

Backtrack immediately you lie.

If you realize that you just added an element of a lie, admit your mistake, apologize, and tell the real truth. When you realize the problem and agree with your partner, you will be adding strength and courage as well as benefits to yourself and the relationships. This action is one of the quickest ways to rebuild trust. Your admittance will give people a new perception about you, and help you start the rebuilding process of getting other people more comfortable with you again step by step.

Even if your admittance leads to anger, don't be discouraged; try to calm the person down instead of creating more excuses to justify your mistakes.

The anger will pass when they notice your sincerity and genuineness. Admitting a lie and confess to your partner immediately and seek their forgiveness can make a lot of difference in your quest to stop lying. This might hurt your pride, but it will cause you to stop and think before you tell another lie.

Note your lies

To monitor the frequency of your lies, and keep track of each occurrence, you can get a notebook that you can carry all the time. On the notebook, indicate the days you deceive people the most and the relating triggers. You can do this continuously for a week or two.

On the notebook, write down all events that trigger the lying episode. Don't forget to include many things like feeling, need or even your regret. What advantage you gain by using deceit and what would have happened if you confront the matter honestly. After about a week or two of writing about such feelings, you can create time to analyze the situation. By this way, you will remember to make the necessary adjustment, fix your lie and never do it again.

Choose the right time for the hurtful truth

If you need to discuss an important matter with your partner and you perceive the truth might hurt him/her. Truth sometimes hurt, but in the end, it brings hope and happiness. Cleverly choose the right time to discuss such a sensitive matter. A time your partner will demonstrate readiness to listen and talk will be ideal. And also find a way to say it in a pleasant way.

Mean your word

During a conversation, if you think you cannot answer a question truthfully at a particular moment. Rather than given evasive and untrue answer you can politely ask for time to reorganize yourself. This is not an attempt to buy time to formulate story but to present yourself in a better and organized way. You will be able to take time and think deeply about what you will say instead of saying something that is not true which you will later regret.

.Be realistic of your ability

Be honest about your ability and what you're capable of doing. Admitting to yourself and your partner about your limitations can help reduce the urge to lie. If you make promises to do something and never intend to follow through, or you don't have the ability to deliver as promised, it is a lie. Inability to deliver makes people look for excuses to cover up. Deliberately broken promises are lies that lead to broken hearts. An open discussion to get everyone to understand your problem will help.

# 7 Ways to Catch a Partner in a Lie

When it comes to detecting lies and deception, there are some subtle physical and behavioral signs that give out a liar to watch for. While open and truthful communication within a relationship is always encouraged. It is imperative to develop the ability to identifying a lying partner and be aware of the reason your partner might lie to you. Understanding the motive is crucial for self-protection. Self-awareness helps to develop the ability to effectively deal with the situation and control the opportunity for the lie to succeed. Refusing to buy into a lie can kill the habit because people continue to lie when they know they easily can get away with it.

Detecting when someone is lying to you isn't always easy, because behavioral differences between honest and lying persons are sometimes difficult to discriminate and measure. But it's important to have this knowledge because even little untruths can slowly erode a relationship. If you suspect that your partner might be lying to you about something in any way, here are some common subtleties that might confirm your suspicions and give away your partner.

Inconsistencies with your partner's stories

Inconsistency and loopholes often characterize a liars' explanation. They can't keep their stories straight. If your partner is explaining a story and you observe that some important elements are left out, or if you notice contradiction and cracks while repeating a story, it can reveal an inconsistency. It is easy to tell if someone is lying if there are inconsistencies in their story because it's difficult to keep track of information that isn't truthful. Usually, they fail to remember details upon retelling or add new information that contradicts the earlier story. Often, liars say what comes to their mind to support their claim. When you suspect lying and deceit, look for irregularities that just don't fit.

Facial hints

We can read a lot about people behavior based on their eye movement especially what the person is feeling. The reason is that the act of lying usually provokes some strong emotions that are difficult to contain. Identifying facial hints is one of closest means that humans can get to mind reading. Deception can show up on your partner's face as a smirk, which would indicate that they've told a lie and believe they're going to get away with it. According to Mark Bouton, an FBI agent for over 30 years and the author of "How to Spot Lies Like the FBI," The ability to read facial expressions to detect lies can be beneficial in identifying a liar in any situation. He says "There are some facial expressions and associated reactions that could indicate someone is lying to you," he says further "Some are caused by nervousness, some by chemical reactions, and others by physical reactions." Some people believe that liars will often touch or cover their mouth and face. It's a distancing mechanism between them and what they're saying.

If your partner is evasive or overreact

If your partner is evasive or overreact to a simple question and try to turn things on you. It could be an indication that something is up especially if this is not how they usually behave. When you directly ask questions they may avoid answering or merely say "I don't know." Being evasive can be a smart way to prevent open the past or fabricate more lies to cover up. Evasion is about trying to change the perception about actions. They are doing this to save their face in the situation because if they avoid answering your questions, you cannot easily pin them down in a lie. Also, using denial phrases repeatedly can be an indication of lying. Denial phrases are evasive.

Using phrases such as "honestly," "trust me," "you know" repeatedly are typical clues to incorrect information.

Body language

There are some bodily signs to look for that can give away a deceiver. Aversion cues such as covering or blocking the mouth or squinting the eyes, covering or rubbing ears or nose can be an indication. Other signs include turning the head or body away when making a crucial statement. Note that, if your partner acts typically in this way when you talk, it may just be his/her normal behavior but when your partner demonstrates inconsistency that should be a red flag.

Fake smile

A 2012 study from British Columbia found that a fake smile often accompanied lying. Liars hide under this to perpetuate their act. A smile that looks odd and doesn't seem quite right, that forms around the mouth but doesn't show around the eyes. The reason is that people find it easier to control the bottom half of their face to force a smile,

## 8 How to Confront a Lying Partner

When you notice that your partner is deliberately deceiving you by doing things that are detrimental to your relationship thereby hurting you and others. When you see a demonstration of a lack of the usual sense of guilt that most people feel when engaging in activities that are morally wrong. Clinically, this type of people are referred to as sociopaths or psychopaths

When you know that you're dealing with deception in your relationship, you need to learn how to manage it productively. There are a few different ways of dealing with this type of problems depending on the root cause.

Confront your partner to discuss the problems in calm; rational manner will help in getting his/her attention. Although, you're in pain, but don't throw it in your partner's face or try to hurt him/her back. In discussing the issue, see it as a conversation and not as a confrontation. Do it in such a way that he/she can hear what you are trying to say without feeling like being attacked. Being listened to and understood is crucial when trying to work through problems with a partner, therefore, avoid open confrontation.

Talk to him/her about your perspectives, your feelings, and your experiences surrounding the lie. Be open and state what's bothering you in the least judgmental way possible. Let him know that you're sad and hurt and that you will appreciate a relationship that isn't hurtful and doesn't include dishonesty.

Don't attack your partner by blaming or point out his misdeeds. But instead, focus on your feelings. Attacking him can make him becoming defensive and may lead to counter attacks, denial, and hostility and lead to other unpredictable consequences. Speak calmly and directly and focus on explaining your feelings about the situation, this may help him to relax and listen to what you have to say since you are not dwelling on his wrongdoing.

You can start by saying, "I found something that is bothering me. I'm disturbed about it, and I wish to discuss it with you."

Tell your partner that you don't want this to happen again in your relationship. Trust is the foundation of love, and you must be able to uphold a healthy sense of trust in one another to maintain a healthy relationship. Using this approach will help you to create a sense of understanding and a willingness to discuss problems without ambiguity.

Once you have entirely stated your feelings and position, allow your partner to speak. Don't interrupt; let him/her express himself/herself freely.

Reassure your partner that he does not have to be anything he's not to impress you. Let him know that you love and value him just as he is. Once you have demonstrated your love for him, you will likely have to confront him with proof of his lies to get him to agree with you that he has a problem. Let him realize the importance of seeking professional help about the issue.

## 9 Ways to Recover From Being Lied to, or Manipulated

The experience of being cheated can be traumatic and leave you emotionally destroyed even long after the experience. It can be very painful to put trust in someone who didn't deserve it. When we found out later we were being deceived we feel betrayed and hurt. Lies told in close relationships will cause a great deal of pain, heartache, and undermine the intimacy and ties you have with your partner.

Research evidence shows that honest people tend to see other people particularly close others, as more honest than they are themselves. And that the more honest we are, the easier we are for manipulators to deceive. Honesty people often trust other people believing that everyone is just like them, a perception which makes them give liars the benefit of the doubt. This makes them more vulnerable to exploitation. Dishonest people are often narcissists who've spent their whole lives learning how to be charming and seem trustworthy looking for people to be exploited.

If you have been cheated by a trusted friend, these are what to do to move on.

Forgive yourself for being fooled.

This may seem hard to do, but you have to move on. Forgive yourself for not being too careful to place your trust in the hand of a deceiver. You have learned your lesson anyway. You need to do some work on yourself and improve your relationship with yourself and also your confidence.

Deal with a known liar cautiously

The chances are that someone who's consistently lied to you is not likely to start being honest just because specific lies have been uncovered. Habit dies hard. Always be aware that a person who once hurts you might take advantage of your good disposition to exploit you again. In dealing with a lying person, you have to act with caution and be more self-protective.

Learn the basics of deception detection.

Learning the basics of deception such as facial expressions, phrases, and behaviors that tend to signal that someone may be lying will help you to be better prepared to deal with a liar. It may not save you totally forever being deceived again but will equip you and take you a step ahead of the game.

Try to check things out

Try to find out the truthfulness of anything you are told by a lying partner. Try to verify any claim and if possible ask for corroboration of any story.

Don't lose your identity

The experience of dealing with a deceitful person can make it very hard not to become a mistrustful person yourself. You may find it extremely difficult to trust anyone and live in suspicion. Viewing the world with suspicion can hurt you more than it benefits you. The truth is that if you have you been hurt in the past, you may find it hard to trust someone again. Don't let the experience change your perception and your right to live and interact with people. But rather deal with people cautiously; see them as trustworthy until they behave otherwise. Don't change who you are.

## How to Trust Again

Betrayal by a loved can be a harrowing experience and make you wonder if you will ever be able to trust anyone again. Feeling bad about it is normal, but the bitter truth is that you may get hurt again someday. There are no guarantees that you won't be hurt in the future. Trust can be compromised by anyone anytime, but the good thing is that it can be developed. Trust is crucial to any meaningful relationships, and you cannot just skip over it. Life loses much of its sparkle and glamour without love and companionship.

If you find it hard to trust someone again here are some things you can do to help you choose to trust again after a painful experience.

Learn to trust yourself

If you don't trust yourself you can't trust others; it starts from you. Trust your judgment and ability to make good choices. Don't ever doubt your ability to make a sound decision for self-growth and sustenance.

Being cheated by a loved one is not a sign of weakness, it does not mean you are a careless individual, or you have a sense of poor judgment. You should not allow the one time experience to hinder your progress.

Reflect on what you have done that has yielded positive results. Good financial good career choices, good health choices, good friendship choices which show you have a strong instinct. Pay attention to your instincts and don't ever doubt your ability, your instincts are powerful.

Review your relationship with the person who broke your trust. If you knew that they would not gain your confidence again, leaving the relationship will be a good option.

## Don't blame yourself

It is natural to blame yourself and feel being fooled and cheated for the behavior of your partner. You should forgive yourself because you have acted with the best intention. Self-forgiveness is essential for you to move on. Remember you are not entirely responsible for the incident, and you can't carry the blame for someone else's actions if you trusted a person with all your heart and turned out to be someone different. For a relationship to thrive and flourish, the two parties must show commitment. If you have acted courageously and done your part faithfully, you should not blame yourself. You are only doing what it is expected of you to make the relationship work.

Leave the past behind you

Because you were once hurt by someone you loved, does not mean that you will not enter into a future relationship. Don't assume that people are the same all over. You have to realize that one person's bad behavior is not a reflection on all humankind. Don't carry over the ugly experience to the future to avoid living in anticipation of another deceit. Don't project the feelings of insecurity onto your new relationship. Otherwise, you may imprisoned yourself and begin to imagine things that don't really exist.

Remember, you deserve to love someone and they deserve your trust. Learn from your experience and stay vigilant for any signs that your past may be influencing how you relate with people. While it is good to avoid the same types of people and situations where your trust was betrayed, you should never let your past experiences taint your future expectations.

Share your experience

When you again do find that perfect person, and you feel ready to trust them, it is important you share your experience and your fear of future heartbreak.

Make your views on trust clear to him/her let them know that you will not put up with any breaking of the trust. It is best to choose to stay open and to trust even after you've been betrayed and hurt. Honesty communication at the beginning of a new relationship promotes mutual understanding.

## 10 Rebuilding a Relationship after Lying

Maintaining trust is essential to having satisfying relationships. Once it is lost in a relationship, it is usually hard to put back together again. Getting it back can sometimes look like an impossible mountain to climb, but repairing the relationship which has been damaged can be possible with determination, commitment, and sincerity from both parties. Both parties must be ready to work at rebuilding the lost trust.

## How to restore your confidence and get your partner to trust you again if You are the Liar

Earning your partner's trust back can prove to be a difficult task, but it is possible. If you realized your mistakes, and you are genuinely remorseful for your actions, you can put in the necessary effort to rebuild the trust you damaged.

Here are some of the things you can do on regaining that trust after you have lost it:

Accepting responsibilities

Note that the situation will not resolve itself without any effort on your part; the first step always has to be admitting your mistakes and apologize. Take some responsibility rather than making excuses, remind yourself what happened and admit your fault. Come clean about the extent of your lies and demonstrate your willingness to work hard to earn back the trust. Avoid covering up or hiding further details to prevent falling into another lie. When the details you are trying to hide eventually come it will only make you look less trustworthy. This fact is crucial because you need to be at peace with yourself before making peace with the people you have deceived.

Apologize and mean it

Apologize, and let your partner know that you regret your action and promise never to do it again. Don't make an empty promise that you cannot follow through. Apologizing and not meaning it will be unfair to your partner, and also to yourself. Tell your partner the exact reason you lied, and explain how things will be different the next time around. Demonstrate and explain your readiness to change and do things differently this time around. Prove that you can be trusted again by following through on your promises and be sincere with your words. To convince your partner of your sincerity act with integrity and let your actions match your words.

## Be honest

Be truthful about whatever you lied about; make sure you're honest about it. For proper amendment and reconciliation, you have to reveal the whole truth to your partner so that he\she can critically assess the situation and react accordingly. Giving the full picture of what actually transpired will allow your partner to make his/her independent assessment rather than being swayed by your opinion. Hiding specific information can worsen the already tensed situation. Your action has already caused considerable damages, so it is better to get it all out of your system and make a proper amendment to heal the wounds and move on. Remain open to talking these issues through, allow your partners to react and express the feelings and distrust which has resulted from your actions or inaction.

Be prepared to be seen as the villain for a while.

After your confession, the trust will not come so easily from your partner. Trust takes time to build. That is the part of the consequences you have to suffer for your mistakes. So be prepared to be seen as the villain until you gradually build the trust with your changed behavior. Accept the consequences of the action that created the hurt and be willing to make a commitment never to hurt your partner again by repeating the hurtful behavior.

Furthermore, don't confuse trust and forgiveness; it will be a mistake to perceive forgiveness as trust being restored. Forgiveness is a gift that is generously given while trust is a privilege that is earned over time. If you have a history of being a repeat offender, you may be forgiven each time you offend and ask for it, but it doesn't mean you are trusted. You have to earn trust by a continuous demonstration of honesty and sincerity in your dealing. Forgiveness allows the offender to work towards trust;

it doesn't mean trust is automatically given. You should know that things may never be quite the same after the horrible experience, but if you show that you are now a trustworthy person, some level of trust can usually be restored.

Allow your partner time to reflect.

Trust rebuilding process takes time; allow your partner time to reflect. Be patient with the healing process as people have different timelines when it comes to healing, and issue of distrust. You have to realize that you can't determine the impact of your action on the victim of your lie. Depending on the severity of your betrayer, it can take a long time to get over and forgive.

Remain calm and compassionate while you await the response of your partner as he/she works to start trusting you once more. But be persistent in your efforts. Remember, it is not mainly about your feelings, you don't have power over this, but you can only influence the outcome through your effort. Understand that issues of distrust may come up again in the future, even when you have convinced yourself the problem is resolved. Learn from your past mistakes and make sure you don't do anything to upset your partner again. Begin to do things perfectly now and don't allow your past to catch up with you again to avoid future problems.

## 11 How to Forgive a Partner Who Hurts You

Keeping an open mind by being able to forgive and to let go, helps to keep you healthy both emotionally and physically. This is a critical tool for developing a healthy relationship. Additionally, the lack of forgiveness is not good for either your mental and physical well-being. Resentment gains momentum and vanishes at the foundation of your relationship. Nursing a perceived hurt can eventually lead to a more severe consequence - hate and extreme bitterness.

Here are some things you can do to get over the problem if you are a victim of deceits.

Be open and receptive to forgiveness.

Accept the reality and be prepared to rebuild the damaged relationship. Come to terms with what happened whenever the other person has shown an effort to make amends for the action. Accept the fact that you've been lied to and make a conscious decision to forgive and prepare to move on. If you keep holding on to old hurts, disappointments, betrayals, and anger, you will not be opened and receptive to forgiveness. Getting all these out of the way clears your mind and frees you from prejudice and hatred. The angrier you are, the less responsive you are to what the other party has to say.

## Consider the apology

Listening to the apology is the most important thing to do. This will give you the opportunity to understand and access the situation and prevent you from making the wrong decision. Try to understand the reason behind the lie will help you clarify whether you can forgive or not. At times the cause can be selfish and insignificant. Sometimes, the reason might actually be rather lofty.

Note that a person who is ready to apologize for wrongdoings without being cruel or defensive is usually genuine. You should, therefore, be welcoming to a person who is trying to correct his mistakes. Accept that you may never know the reason for the behavior or mistake and be ready to consider the apology.

Express yourself

For complete reconciliation it is essential you express your feelings, talk about what you have passed through as a result of the hurtful behavior. If necessary, allow yourself to be emotional let out those tears that you've been holding on. This is important to make the other party see the damage they have caused you.

Take your time in deciding how to react

You don't need to hurry the process. You may not conclude right away. Be patient with yourself. And don't make any rash decisions you might regret further down the line. Assess the situation critically and take time to react. You need to know if the request is coming from a penitent heart or another form of deception. Try to understand if the person feels actually sorry for hurting you and demonstrate a genuine readiness for amendment.

Forgive and move on

Forgive and move on when you are satisfied with your findings. Do not throw a mistake back in your partners face at a later date, learn to forgive and forget. When images of the hurtful behavior flash in your mind, think of something to distract yourself from dwelling on those thoughts. You don't have to always treat your partner as a liar, "Once a cheater, always a cheater" is not necessarily true. But always be aware that a person who hurts you might take advantage of your good nature. Do not seek out for revenge or retribution, trying to get even will only aggravate the pain.

Relationships, need forgiveness to thrive, everyone makes mistakes we need to forgive and to be forgiven. Even though you may find it find it pretty difficult to forgive, being able to do so is crucial for your relationship to be sustained over a long period. It can be hard to forgive a person who deceived you. It takes some reflection, forbearance, problem-solving, and a good deal of communication with your partner.

## Conclusion

Lying does nothing good for a relationship, no matter which way you may try to spin it. It is a temporary solution to a permanent problem. Lying doesn't solve anything; it only prolongs issues and makes the situation worse. Whenever you are tempted to lie, try and think of the aversive consequence and make honesty with your partner a conscious decision and a regular habit. The effects of lying always outweigh the short term benefit. When you practice speaking the truth in small things, it makes telling big lies less easy. No matter the situation, you should never lie to someone you love. Honesty is as vital to your relationship as love. The bigger the lie, the more the hazard it portends to your relationship. Love is meant to be an instrument of sincerity, openness, and integrity enabling us to grow together. Lying contradicts everything that love stands for. When we lie to each other, we can't grow together.

## About the author

David has over 25 years professional experience working as a trainer, counselor, motivator, and administrator. He loves to help people change their lives and achieve their goals in life. David has written or edited a dozen of books where he shares practical techniques that anyone can use to make the desired changes in their lives.

# References and Books for Further Reading

David Joseph, 2018, How to Stop compulsive Lying, Amazon Kindle

Debbie Davids , 2017, How to stop Lying, Amazon Kindle.

Mark Bouton ( 2010), How to Spot Lies Like the FBI, Cosmic Wind Press

Meyer, P. (2011). *Liespotting: Proven techniques to detect deception.* New York: NY: St. Martin's Griffin

Gigy, L., & Kelly, J. B. 1993, Reasons for divorce: Perspectives of divorcing men and women. *Journal of Divorce and Remarriage.*

DePaulo, B.M. et. al. 2003. Cues to Deception. Psychological Bulletin

Bering, J. 2011, 18 Attributes of Highly Effective Liars. Scientific American

Ford, Charles V. 1996. Lies!, Lies!, Lies!: the Psychology of Deceit. Washington, D.C.: American Psychiatric Press. Inc.

Warren, G., Schertler, E., & Bull, P. 2009. Detecting deception from emotional and unemotional cues. Journal of Nonverbal Behavior.

Navarro, Joe. 2008. What Every Body Is Saying. New York: Harper Collins.

Drefahl, S. 2012,. Do the married really live longer? The role of cohabitation and socioeconomic status. *Journal of Marriage and Family.*

Gino, F., & Bazeman, M. H. 2009, When misconduct goes unnoticed: *Journal of Experimental and Social Psychology.*

Savedge, J. 2016. Being in a healthy relationship may help you live longer

Made in United States
North Haven, CT
24 September 2022

24515999R00065